PICTUREPEDIA

NOTE TO PARENTS

This book is part of PICTUREPEDIA, a completely
new kind of information series for children.
Its unique combination of pictures and words
encourages children to use their eyes to discover and
explore the world, while introducing them to a wealth
of basic knowledge. Clear, straightforward text
explains each picture thoroughly and provides
additional information about the topic.

'Looking it up' becomes an easy task with
PICTUREPEDIA, an ideal first reference for all types of
schoolwork. Because PICTUREPEDIA is also entertaining,
children will enjoy reading its words and looking
at its pictures over and over again. You can encourage
and stimulate further inquiry by helping your child
pose simple questions for the whole family to
'look up' and answer together.

YOUR
BODY

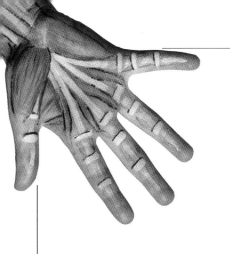

DK

A DORLING KINDERSLEY BOOK

Conceived, edited and designed by DK Direct Limited

Consultant Dr Fiona Payne

Writer Jean Rustean
Editor Sarah Miller
Art Editor Sara Nunan
Designer Tuong Nguyen

Series Editor Sarah Phillips
Series Art Editor Paul Wilkinson

Picture Researcher Paul Snelgrove

Production Manager Ian Paton

Editorial Director Jonathan Reed
Design Director Ed Day

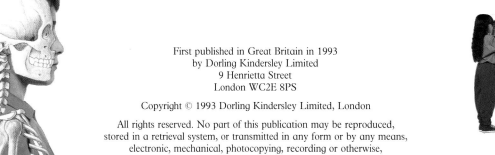

First published in Great Britain in 1993
by Dorling Kindersley Limited
9 Henrietta Street
London WC2E 8PS

A CIP catalogue record for this
book is available from the British Library.

ISBN 0-7513-5041-9

Reproduced by Colourscan, Singapore
Printed and bound in Italy by Graphicom

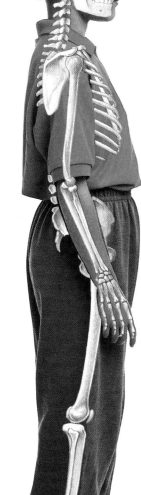

YOUR BODY

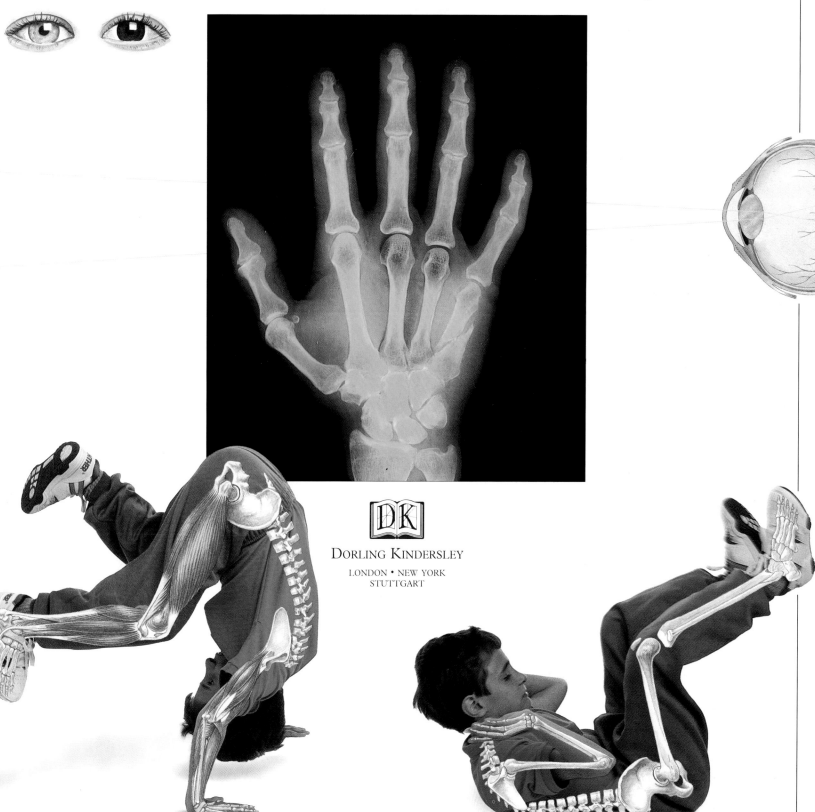

DK

DORLING KINDERSLEY

LONDON • NEW YORK
STUTTGART

CONTENTS

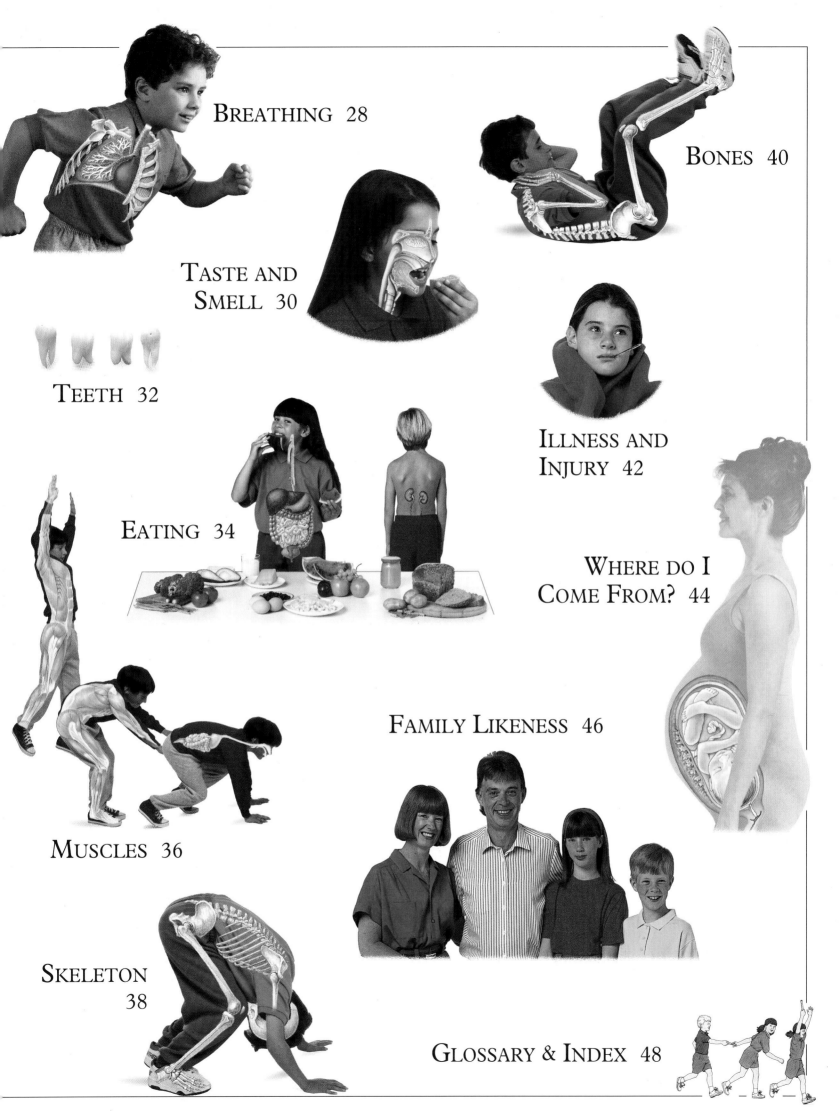

INSIDE YOUR BODY

Your body is one of the most amazing machines in the world. Like a car, it is made up of thousands of parts all working together. Each group of parts is called a system. The body is so complicated that it is sometimes easier to think about the different systems separately. Because they all work together, you could not live with only some of the systems – you need all of them to stay alive.

Skeleton
Over two hundred bones are linked together to make your body's framework. It is called your skeleton. It supports your body and protects all the delicate bits inside you.

Digestive System
The food you eat has to be turned into fuel for your body to use as energy. Your digestive system chops up the food, breaks it down and absorbs the useful parts.

You have 12 pairs of ribs in your body. How many can you feel?

Your spine is made up of lots of small bones.

Your small intestine is probably starting to digest your breakfast as you begin your lunch.

Your pelvis is made of two wide, flat bones.

Once the food reaches your large intestine most of the goodness has already been taken from it.

The largest bone in your body is the thigh bone, or femur.

The largest joint in your body is your knee.

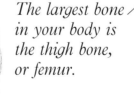

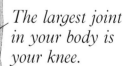

Your foot has 26 separate bones.

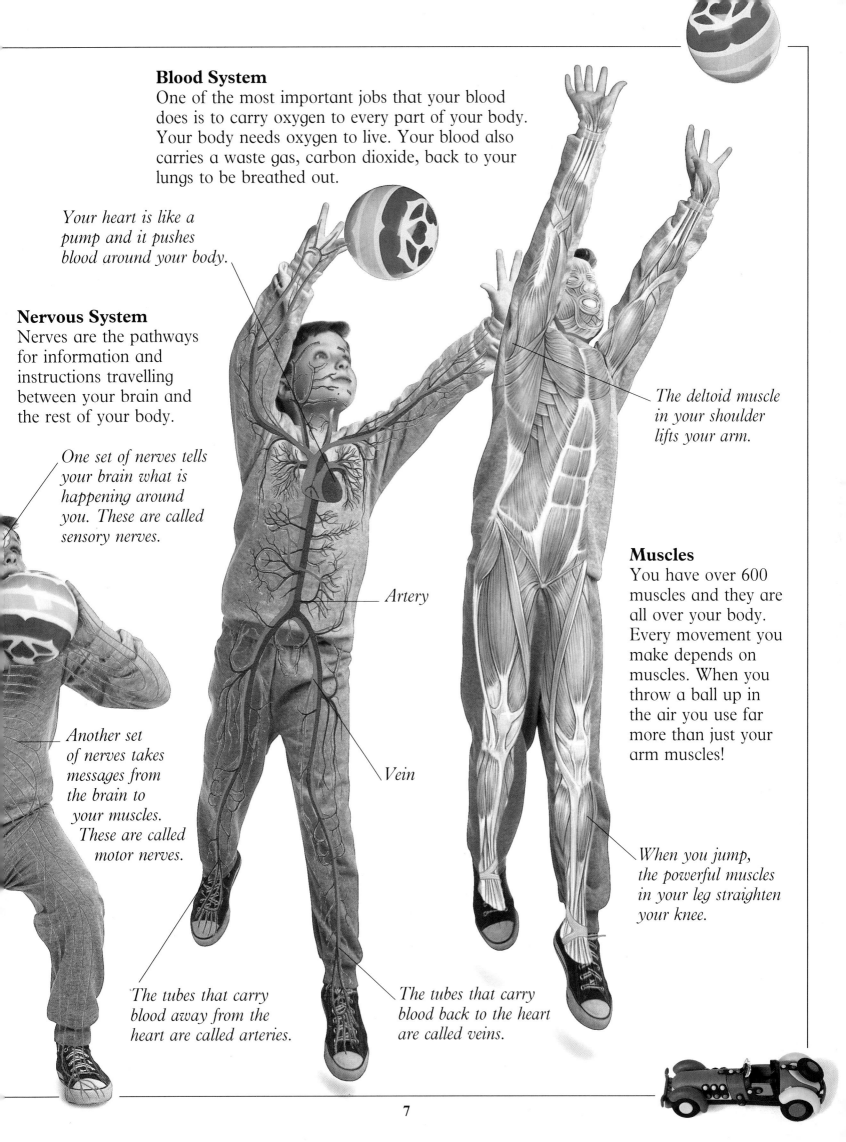

Blood System
One of the most important jobs that your blood does is to carry oxygen to every part of your body. Your body needs oxygen to live. Your blood also carries a waste gas, carbon dioxide, back to your lungs to be breathed out.

Your heart is like a pump and it pushes blood around your body.

Nervous System
Nerves are the pathways for information and instructions travelling between your brain and the rest of your body.

One set of nerves tells your brain what is happening around you. These are called sensory nerves.

Another set of nerves takes messages from the brain to your muscles. These are called motor nerves.

Artery

Vein

The deltoid muscle in your shoulder lifts your arm.

Muscles
You have over 600 muscles and they are all over your body. Every movement you make depends on muscles. When you throw a ball up in the air you use far more than just your arm muscles!

When you jump, the powerful muscles in your leg straighten your knee.

The tubes that carry blood away from the heart are called arteries.

The tubes that carry blood back to the heart are called veins.

SKILLS

As you grow older you learn to do more difficult things. It takes time to discover how all the parts of your body can move and to get them to work together. You have to learn how to thread beads or turn a cartwheel. For you to balance properly, your brain has to take messages from your eyes, muscles, joints and even your ears!

Up or Down?

Inside each of your ears there are three fluid-filled tubes, called semi-circular canals. When your head moves, the liquid moves too. Small hairs in the tubes detect this movement and send signals to the brain telling it which way up you are.

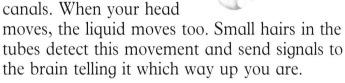

Dizzy Brain
If you spin round and round and then stop, you feel giddy. This is because the liquid in your ears is still swirling round, so the message to your brain is that you are still moving. But your eyes are telling your brain that you have stopped moving, so your brain cells become confused and you feel very dizzy.

When you turn a cartwheel you don't have to think about every movement you must make. Your brain tells your body which muscles to use.

Your eyes spot the next position for your hands.

Your brain has instructed the muscles in your foot and leg to push your body over.

Crawling
(about 10
months)

Walking
(about 15
months)

Hopping
(about 4
years)

Skipping
(about 5
years)

Riding a two-
wheeled bicycle
(about 5 years)

Better Balanced

As you grow older you gain more control
over your muscles and are able to do more
difficult things with your body. Watching
a baby learning to crawl and walk you see
how hard they have to try.

*Your muscles receive messages
from your brain telling them
which movements are needed
to keep your balance, and
to prepare for landing.*

Rope Walk

This tightrope walker has spent many
hours practising. If he starts to lean over
one way he will move the pole the other
way to help him to keep his balance.

*Your foot will make
small adjustments
when it lands to help
you to stay upright.*

*Your brain
knows the
position of
your body.*

FACE

You can recognize hundreds of people just by looking at their faces. As well as your family and friends, think of all the people you see on television and recognize at once. Faces are very special and they are nearly all different, even though they all have the same basic features. By changing expressions, your face can show how you are feeling.

Up and Down Brows

The position of your eyebrows changes your facial expression.

Raised eyebrows give a look of surprise.

A frown uses over 40 face muscles!

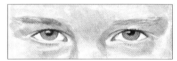

Eyebrows in normal resting position.

Raise one eyebrow at a time for a questioning look.

A Sad Smile

If you draw a smile or a frown on your face with make up, you make it harder for people to see your real feelings.

Learn to Girn

Over one hundred muscles let you pull all sorts of faces. Some people enter girning competitions – to see who can make the most unusual face.

Face in Place

When people talk to you they look mainly at your face. This is because your face tells other people what you are feeling. A very small baby can really only focus on faces. When young children draw pictures of people they usually start by drawing a face which has legs and arms, but no body at all. This shows that, to a very young child, the face represents the whole person.

Half and Half

The two sides of your face are not exactly the same! This boy's left ear sticks out more than the right. The two sides of his nose are not the same either. So if the right side of his face is reflected onto the left, it makes his whole face look different. You can try this for yourself by holding a mirror vertically down the centre of a photograph of your face. Which side do you prefer?

Two right sides

Two left sides

You raise your eyebrows by tensing the muscles in your forehead.

When you smile you use about 15 muscles – a lot fewer than it takes to frown!

Your eyes show that you are smiling.

There are eleven muscles on each side of your mouth. These allow your mouth and lips to make shapes so that you can talk, eat, frown or smile.

VOICE

Your voice is your main method of communicating with other people. You can often recognize people by just hearing the sound of their voice. Voices can be loud or soft, squeaky or deep, harsh or musical. You can use your voice to speak, sing, shout, laugh or cry. All these sounds are made by your voice box, or larynx, as you breathe out. From the moment you are born you can communicate your needs by crying, but it is not until you are over one year old that you learn how to make these sounds into words.

Tongue Tied
Your tongue is very important when you are talking. What happens if you try to speak while holding your tongue?

Stretch and Relax
Inside the voice box there are two stretchy vocal cords. When you breathe out, air passes between these cords, causing them to vibrate. Like the neck of a balloon when air is let out, the vocal cords make different sounds as they stretch in different ways.

Sound Shapers
The voice box makes sounds, but you need your mouth, tongue, lips and teeth to make the sounds into letters and words.

Your voice box, or larynx, shows up on the outside of your throat as your Adam's apple. You can feel it vibrate as you speak.

Vocal cords

Foodpipe, or gullet

Windpipe, or trachea

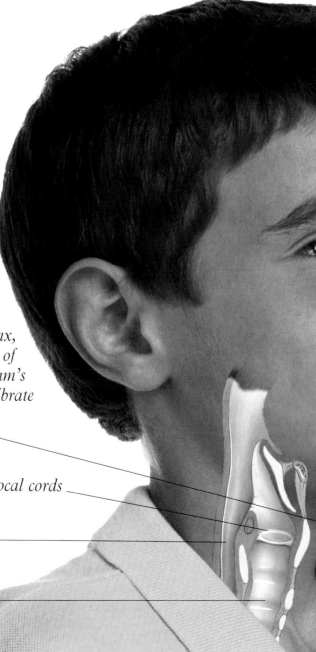

'How much wood could a woodchuck chop if a woodchuck could chop wood'

Tongue Twister

Some groups of words can be tricky to say. Try saying this sentence about a woodchuck!

Throwing Your Voice

Keep your mouth still, and with your lips slightly apart, talk for your puppet. Which sounds and words are harder to say than others? Try saying 'Parrots can fly'. People who have learned to do this very well are called ventriloquists.

From High to Low

Boys sing with high voices, often until they are teenagers. As they grow, their vocal cords grow too. Their muscles find it hard to control these bigger cords and their voice wobbles from high to low – it is 'breaking'. When their muscles have adjusted, their voice becomes deeper.

 Mmmm

 Ooooh

 Eeeeh

 Aaaah

Mouth Moves

Look in a mirror and watch your mouth while you say these sounds. Try saying 'Aaaah' with your lips closed!

The harder you breathe out, the louder the sounds are that you can make.

When you whisper you cannot feel your Adam's apple vibrate.

Talk Time

Take a deep breath and then time yourself talking normally until you run out of breath. Now take another deep breath and shout at the top of your voice. Can you shout for the same amount of time? Which makes you run out of breath faster, talking or shouting?

HEARING

Hearing is one of your five senses. Your ears are important and delicate: they pick up sounds and send messages to your brain. Sounds travel through the air in waves. Your outer ears, the shell-shaped flaps on the side of your head, catch sound waves and funnel them inside. These waves hit the eardrum and make it vibrate. The middle ear and the inner ear change the vibrations into electrical signals, which are sorted out and recognized by your brain.

T

X

I

B

The outer ear collects the sounds and funnels them along the ear canal.

Crash!
The loudness of sound is measured in decibels. Quiet whispering is less than 25 decibels, the clash of cymbals about 90 and a jet plane taking off can measure more than 130 decibels. Noises over 120 decibels can cause pain and may damage your ears.

Talking in Signs
If deaf people have never heard speech, they may not have learned to talk. To help them to communicate, many learn a special language called signing. They also learn to spell using their hands, and to lip-read by watching the shape of people's mouths as they speak.

Three tiny, connected bones in the middle ear – the hammer, anvil and stirrup – pass sound vibrations from the eardrum to the cochlea.

The semi-circular canals help you balance.

Nerves

Hello . . . Hello!
If you shout in a large, empty space, the sound waves from your voice bounce off the nearest surface, back to your ears. This is called an echo. The further a sound has to travel before it is reflected, the longer you must wait for the echo.

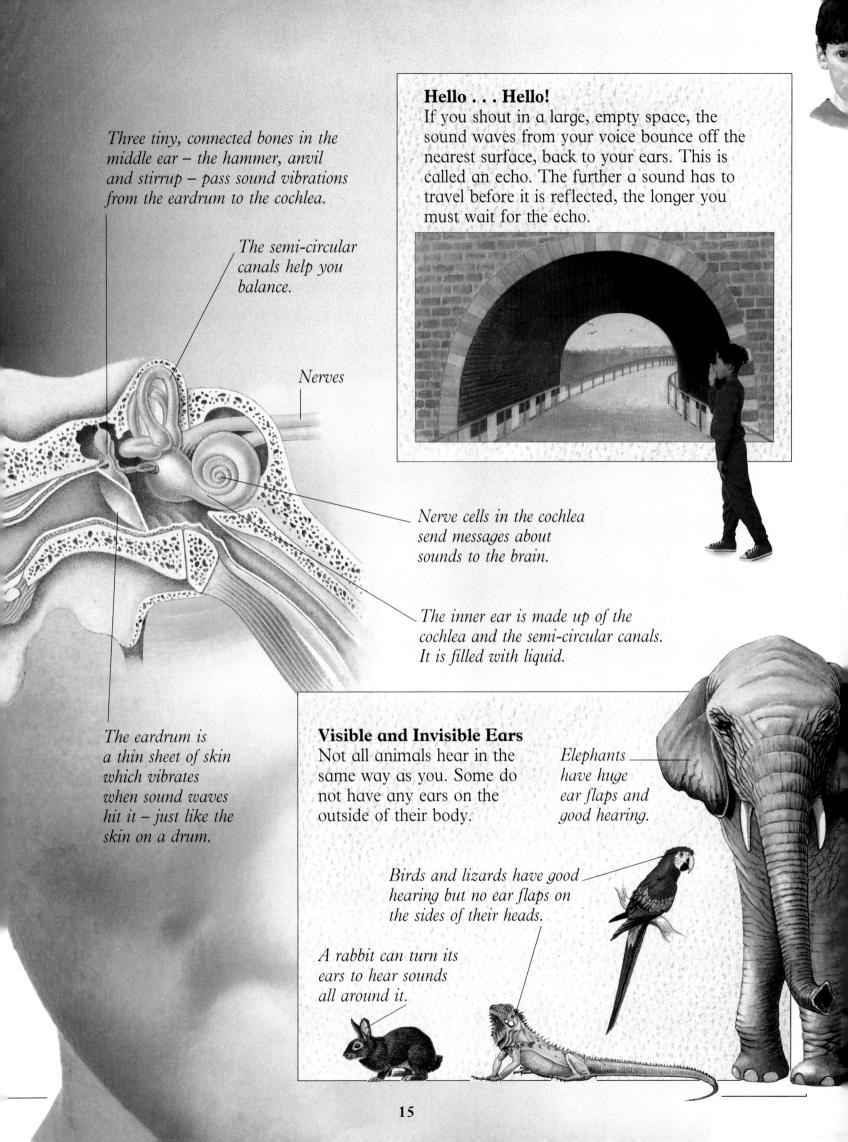

Nerve cells in the cochlea send messages about sounds to the brain.

The inner ear is made up of the cochlea and the semi-circular canals. It is filled with liquid.

The eardrum is a thin sheet of skin which vibrates when sound waves hit it – just like the skin on a drum.

Visible and Invisible Ears
Not all animals hear in the same way as you. Some do not have any ears on the outside of their body.

Elephants have huge ear flaps and good hearing.

Birds and lizards have good hearing but no ear flaps on the sides of their heads.

A rabbit can turn its ears to hear sounds all around it.

SEEING

Tear-Full
Tears help to keep your eyes moist and clean. When too many are made, they cannot all drain away down your nose, so tears come out of your eyes.

Sight is perhaps the most important of your five senses. Your eyes work together with your brain to help you to see. The cornea, at the front of your eye, bends light. This light is then focused by the lens, to form an image of what you are looking at on the retina at the back of your eye. But the image is upside down! Nerve cells in the retina send messages to your brain, which sorts the messages out so that you see things the right way up.

Tricky Eyes
Sometimes your eyes play tricks on you, called optical illusions. Try these:

Which of these two girls is the taller?

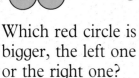

Which red circle is bigger, the left one or the right one?

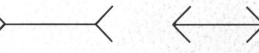

Which line is longer?

Double Vision?
Because they are set apart, each of your eyes sees a slightly different picture. Your brain puts the two pictures together. This is called stereoscopic or binocular vision, and it means you can judge depth and distances. Try this: close one eye, point to something and keep your finger still. Now look through the other eye. Are you still pointing to the same place?

Eye Spy
You can have your eyes tested by an optometrist to make sure they are working properly. Glasses or contact lenses will help if you cannot see clearly. Your eyes are very important so have them checked regularly!

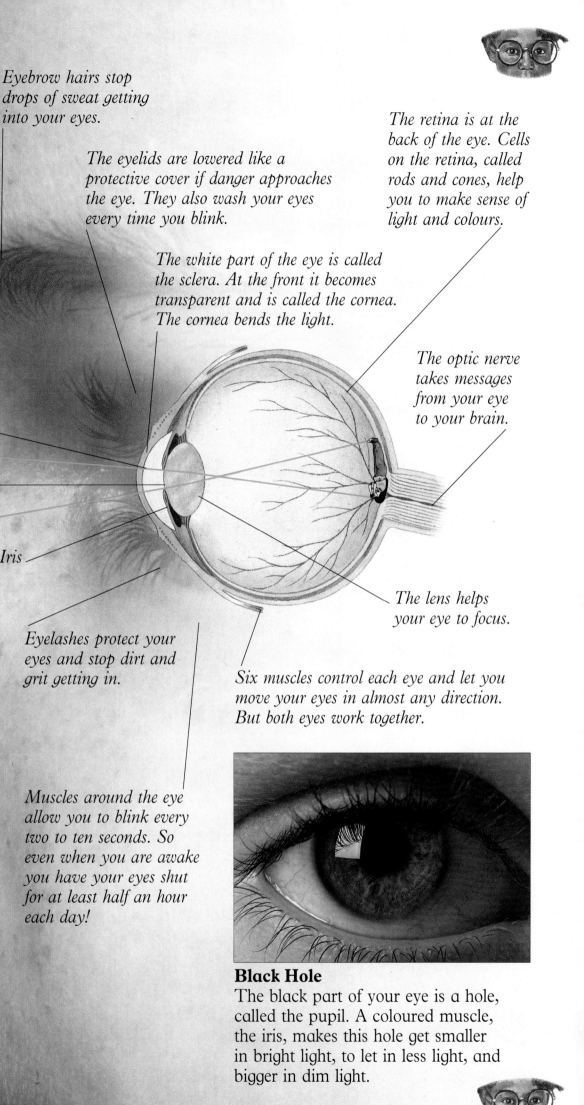

Eyebrow hairs stop drops of sweat getting into your eyes.

The eyelids are lowered like a protective cover if danger approaches the eye. They also wash your eyes every time you blink.

The retina is at the back of the eye. Cells on the retina, called rods and cones, help you to make sense of light and colours.

The white part of the eye is called the sclera. At the front it becomes transparent and is called the cornea. The cornea bends the light.

The conjunctiva is transparent, like a window. It protects the front of your eye.

The optic nerve takes messages from your eye to your brain.

Light enters the eye through the pupil.

Iris

The lens helps your eye to focus.

Eyelashes protect your eyes and stop dirt and grit getting in.

Six muscles control each eye and let you move your eyes in almost any direction. But both eyes work together.

Muscles around the eye allow you to blink every two to ten seconds. So even when you are awake you have your eyes shut for at least half an hour each day!

Black Hole
The black part of your eye is a hole, called the pupil. A coloured muscle, the iris, makes this hole get smaller in bright light, to let in less light, and bigger in dim light.

BRAIN

Inside your head, protected by a bony skull, is your brain. It looks crinkled like a walnut and is the control centre for the whole of your body. Your heart pumps oxygen-filled blood into it through a mass of tubes, called arteries. After only four minutes without oxygen, brain cells will die and they cannot be replaced. Your brain is divided into two halves, called hemispheres. Each half controls different activities.

Top Gear
To stop you injuring your brain, you should wear a helmet whenever you take part in a sport that might make you knock your head.

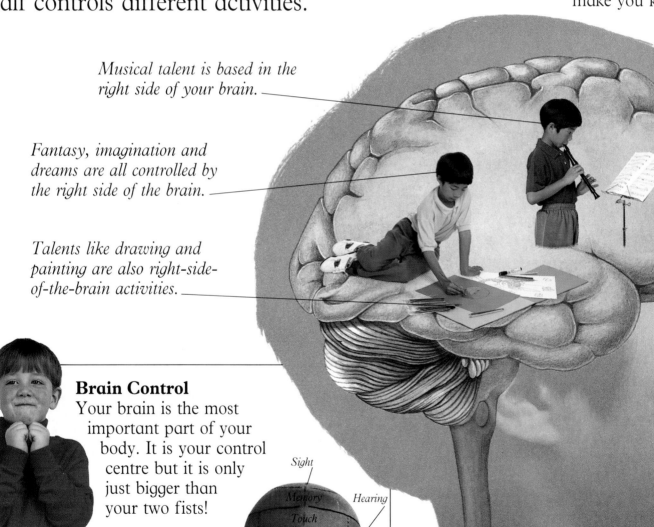

Musical talent is based in the right side of your brain.

Fantasy, imagination and dreams are all controlled by the right side of the brain.

Talents like drawing and painting are also right-side-of-the-brain activities.

Brain Control
Your brain is the most important part of your body. It is your control centre but it is only just bigger than your two fists!

Sight
Memory
Hearing
Touch
Hearing
Movement
Speech
Personality

Signals coming in and going out to other parts of your body, such as your eyes, mouth, ears and skin, are all controlled by different areas of your brain.

Kim's Game

When we are learning we depend on our memory to help us. Test your memory with this game. Set out a number of objects and look at them for a few moments. Ask a friend to remove an object then try to tell what is missing.

Different Brains

Animals have brains of various shapes and sizes, suited to the things they do.

Fish

Bird

Cat

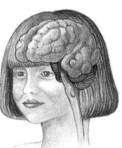

Human

Mathematical and logical problems are sorted out by the left side of your brain.

Your right arm is controlled by the left side of your brain.

The left side of your brain remembers names, dates and facts.

The left side of your brain controls language skills. It enables you to speak, read and write.

The brain stem controls many of your automatic actions, such as your heartbeat and breathing.

Brain Relay

When you want to touch something, a signal is passed from your brain to other parts of your body like a baton in a relay race. It goes first to the spinal nerves then to the motor nerves, which tell muscles to move.

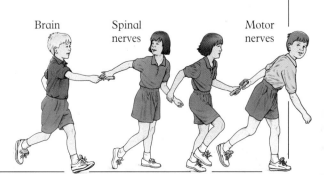

Brain · Spinal nerves · Motor nerves

Left, Right, Left
The ideas in these two large pictures are thought to be true for right-handed people. In left-handed people they may be reversed.

19

NERVES

Nerves are like telephone cables carrying information between the brain and all parts of the body. One set of nerves – the sensory nerves – carries signals to your brain from your senses, telling your brain what is happening around you. When your brain has decided what to do it sends signals along another set of nerves – the motor nerves – to make your muscles work.

Nerve network

Speedy Reflex
If someone claps their hands by your face your brain thinks something is flying towards your eyes and they blink. This blink is a reflex action to protect them.

With your eyes covered, can you tell it is a teddy bear?

What's on the 'Feely Table'?
The sense of touch is very important. It is one of your five senses. Receptor cells under your skin send messages, through sensory nerves, to your brain about what your fingers are feeling.

A bottle feels hard and smooth.

Reading by Touch
Blind people cannot see to read so they learn a special alphabet of raised dots, called braille. They feel these dots with their fingertips.

Get the Message?
Messages about how objects feel are sent through the sensory nerves and the spinal nerves to the brain to be understood.

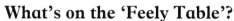

Sensory nerves   Spinal nerves   Brain

If you touch some honey, your fingers will find that it is sticky.

Ice is cold and slippery. When it starts to melt it feels wet.

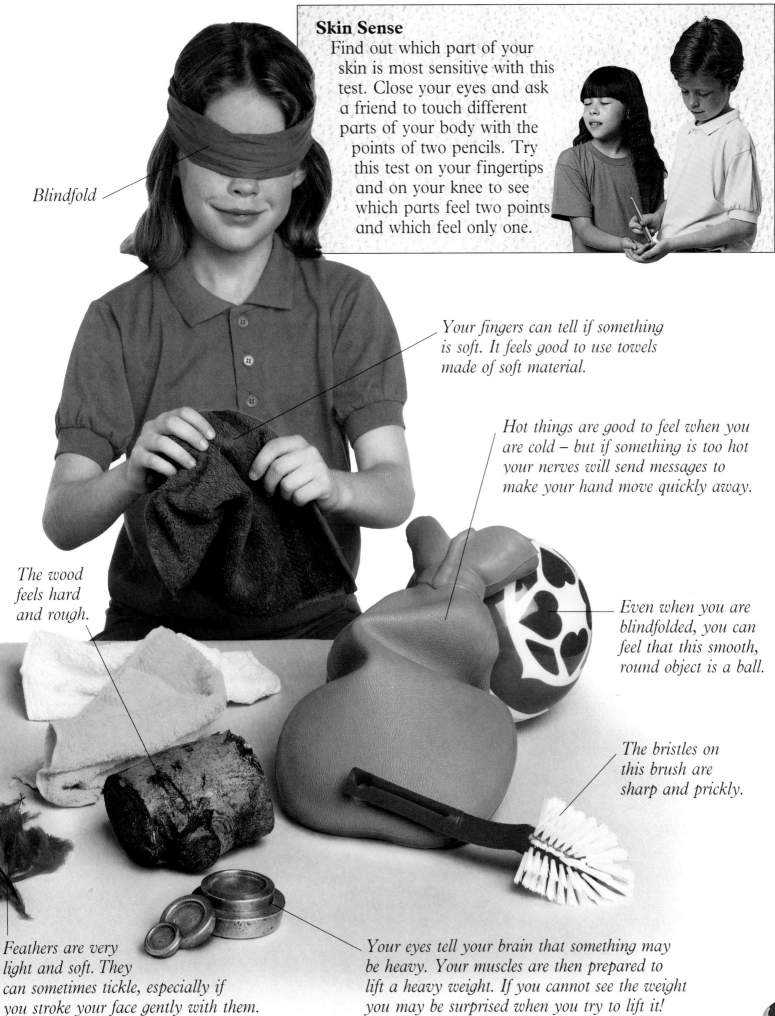

Skin Sense
Find out which part of your skin is most sensitive with this test. Close your eyes and ask a friend to touch different parts of your body with the points of two pencils. Try this test on your fingertips and on your knee to see which parts feel two points and which feel only one.

Blindfold

Your fingers can tell if something is soft. It feels good to use towels made of soft material.

Hot things are good to feel when you are cold – but if something is too hot your nerves will send messages to make your hand move quickly away.

The wood feels hard and rough.

Even when you are blindfolded, you can feel that this smooth, round object is a ball.

The bristles on this brush are sharp and prickly.

Feathers are very light and soft. They can sometimes tickle, especially if you stroke your face gently with them.

Your eyes tell your brain that something may be heavy. Your muscles are then prepared to lift a heavy weight. If you cannot see the weight you may be surprised when you try to lift it!

SKIN

If you could unwrap your skin, you might be surprised at how much you have – enough to cover a large towel. It goes over all your bumps and curves and into every crease of your body. Your skin grows with you, so that when you are an adult it will cover an area of about 1.7 square metres. It is waterproof and protective and can heal itself if it gets damaged.

New skin grows all the time to replace old skin that rubs off. Most house dust is really old, dead skin!

The thinnest skin is on your eyelids.

Personal Prints

Fingerprints are patterns of lines and swirls on your fingers. Try printing yours using paint or ink! Everyone has different fingerprints so they are used to identify people. There are three basic patterns.

Hairs grow on every part of your skin except for your lips, the palms of your hands and the soles of your feet.

Arch

Loop

Whorl

A fingernail takes about six months to grow from base to tip. It grows about half a millimetre a week.

Nails are made of dead cells which contain a protein called keratin.

The cuticle is the fold of skin overlapping the nail-bed from where the nail grows.

The half-moon at the base of your nail looks white because this part is not firmly attached to the skin below.

Shades

All skin contains a colouring substance called melanin. Dark skin contains more melanin than fair skin. As a protection from burning by the Sun, the skin produces more melanin which tans the skin a darker colour.

The roots of your hair are alive and grow about two millimetres a week. When the hairs reach the surface of your skin they die – so having your hair cut does not hurt!

Growing Old

Your skin is elastic. If you pinch the back of your hand and then release it, the skin goes back to its original place. As people get older their skin becomes less elastic and often gets wrinkled. Some people's hair turns grey because it stops making melanin.

Dead or Alive?

Your skin has two layers. The dead, outer layer, called the epidermis, protects the living dermis underneath.

Hair

A pore is the opening of a sweat gland.

Epidermis

Dermis

Nerve ending

Oil glands stop skin drying out

Hair follicle

Sweat glands / *open to let moisture out of your skin to help keep you cool.*

Blood vessels bring food and oxygen to the skin.

Hair Styles

How straight or curly a hair is depends upon the shape of the pocket, or follicle, it grows from. The colour of your hair depends upon the amount of black or red melanin there is inside these pockets.

TEMPERATURE

Your body is able to make its own heat so that it can stay at about the same temperature all the time. The normal temperature of your body is about 37 °C. This is controlled by your brain, but it is the sweat glands and blood vessels in the surface of your skin which make the many minute-by-minute changes. When you are hot, sweat glands cool you down and when you begin to feel cold, blood vessels shrink to warm you up.

Top-Up
When your body loses a lot of water – because the weather is very hot or you have been exercising – you must replace it by drinking.

Heat loss — Sweat — Sweat gland

Hot Under the Collar
As the temperature of your body rises, sweat from your sweat glands comes to the surface of your skin. As this moisture dries, it takes some of the heat away.

After strenuous exercise, make sure that you do some gentle cooling-down exercises. This lets your muscles ease back into their cool resting positions.

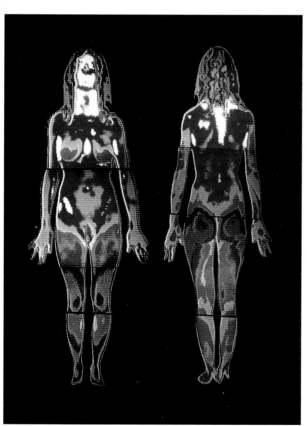

White Hot
These pictures show the temperature of a woman's body. The white parts are the hottest. Next hottest are the red parts, then the orange, green, blue and finally, the cold purple feet.

When you are hot, your blood vessels open up to let blood flow nearer to the surface of your skin. This helps you cool down.

Energy Break

When the weather is cold, your body uses up a lot of energy in order to keep warm. This means you need to eat more to replace the energy. Polar explorers have to carry lots of food with them on expeditions and they stop often to eat.

Keep your head covered in cold weather because three quarters of the heat that escapes from your body does so through your head.

Hair

Erector muscle

Chilly Bumps

Goose bumps appear on your body because the cold makes the small hairs stand on end. The muscles of these hairs work without instructions from your brain. Each bump shows where a hair is growing. The hairs trap a layer of warm air next to the skin, but because we are not covered in thick hair it does not keep us that warm.

You shiver when your muscles are trying to make extra heat by working on their own. As they quickly tighten and relax, your body trembles.

In cold weather you should wear lots of layers of clothes. Warm air will get trapped between your coat, jumper and T-shirt, keeping your body warm.

BLOOD

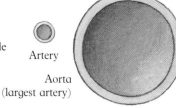

Arteriole Artery

Aorta
(largest artery)

Blood is pumped all around your body by your heart. It travels in long tubes called blood vessels. Before it begins this journey, it is pushed to your lungs to collect oxygen. Then it returns to your heart to be pumped around your body. Blood also carries nutrients from your food to the cells.

There . . .
Blood vessels that take blood away from your heart are called arteries.

Power Pump
Your heart is made of strong muscle. In just one minute, it can pump a drop of blood all the way down to your toes and back to your heart again.

The heart is divided into four spaces called chambers, two at the top and two at the bottom. There is a wall of muscle down the middle.

Blood enters the top right chamber through the vena cava. It passes down to the bottom right chamber. Then it is pushed out to your lungs.

Blood, filled with oxygen from the lungs, comes into the top left chamber. It passes down to the bottom left chamber. Then it is pumped around your body.

After going around your body, the blood returns to the right side of your heart, to start the journey again.

Aorta

Flaps, called valves, stop blood from flowing the wrong way. It is the 'lub-dub' sound of these doors closing that you hear when your heart beats.

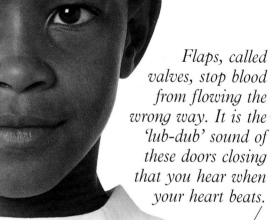

Venule Vein

Vena cava
(largest vein)

... and Back
Those that take blood
back to your heart are
called veins.

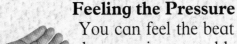

Feeling the Pressure
You can feel the beat of your
heart as it pumps blood, at high
pressure, through your arteries.
This beat is called the pulse. Put
the fingers of one hand on the inside
of your other wrist, in line with your thumb.
You can feel your pulse beating there. You
can only hear a
heartbeat by using
a stethoscope or by
putting your ear
to a friend's chest.

Heart Work
When you skip, or take any
form of exercise, your muscles
need extra oxygen and food
from your blood. To provide this,
your heart has to pump faster.

*You have about four litres
of blood in your body. An adult
has more and a baby has less.*

*A drop of blood goes round your
body more than a thousand times
a day. Every five minutes all your
blood passes through your kidneys
to be cleaned.*

Super Cells
In one tiny drop of blood
there are red cells, white
cells and platelets, all floating
in a liquid called plasma.
The blood in your arteries is
carrying oxygen which makes
it a brighter red colour than
the blood in your veins.

Side view of a
red blood cell

*Red cells carry oxygen
around the body. They are
made in the bone marrow.*

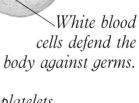

*White blood
cells defend the
body against germs.*

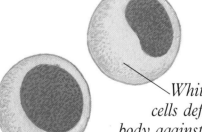

*If you cut yourself, platelets
rush to the broken blood
vessel and stick themselves
together to plug the hole.*

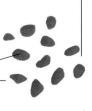

BREATHING

You must breathe all the time to stay alive. If you try to hold your breath for more than about a minute your body will force you to start breathing again. The air that you breathe is made up of many different gases mixed together, but your body only needs one of them, oxygen, to keep you alive. If you ran out of oxygen, even for a very short time, you would die. The air you breathe goes into two soft, moist sponges, called lungs. You have one on each side of your chest.

Lung Capacity
Breathe in deeply. Blow into a balloon until you run out of breath. Tie a knot in the balloon. Now you can see just how much air your lungs are able to hold.

Bad Breath!
The air that you breathe can contain gases that are bad for you. This woman is wearing a mask to protect herself from car fumes.

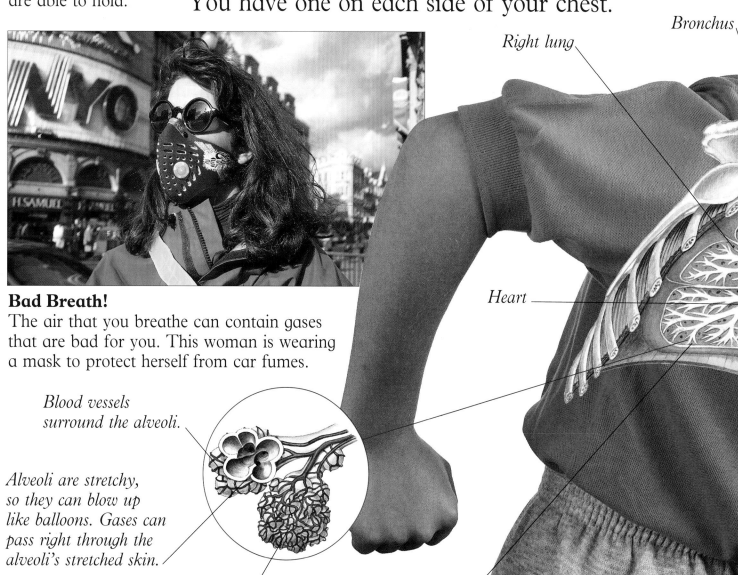

Right lung

Bronchus

Heart

Blood vessels surround the alveoli.

Alveoli are stretchy, so they can blow up like balloons. Gases can pass right through the alveoli's stretched skin.

Oxygen seeps from the alveoli into the blood. A waste gas, called carbon dioxide, seeps from the blood back into the alveoli to be breathed out.

Some air is always left in your lungs because they would collapse if they were completely empty.

You breathe air in through a tube called the windpipe, or trachea.

Hot Air

The air that you breathe out is warm and has water in it. You can see this if you breathe onto a mirror. The water in your breath cools down and forms a mist as it hits the cold mirror. If you touch the mirror you can feel the moisture. You can also see the water misting-up when you breathe out on a cold day.

Air enters the lungs through two large tubes called the bronchi. Each bronchus divides into smaller and smaller tubes ending in tiny sacs called alveoli.

Your ribs form a cage. They protect your lungs.

Breathe In

A powerful muscle, called the diaphragm, helps you breathe air into both your lungs. When this muscle is pulled tight, it moves downwards, leaving more space for the lungs. As the lungs spread out to fill this larger space, they suck in air.

Breathe Out

When your diaphragm relaxes, it moves back up again and squashes your lungs. There is no longer enough space in your lungs for all the air, so it is squeezed up your windpipe and out of your nose or mouth.

Mucus

Dirt

Tiny 'hairs' trap dirt.

Little 'brushes' help to push dirt out of your body.

Special cells

Wall of the bronchus

Sneezing

A sudden rush of built-up air blows dust or germs from your nose.

Coughing

Dust or germs in the tubes of your lungs are forced out quickly.

Laughing

The diaphragm jerks, forcing air up through your voice box and windpipe.

TASTE AND SMELL

Your senses of taste and smell are very closely linked. They depend on each other. Tiny dimples on your tongue, and hairs at the top of the inside of your nose, detect chemicals that cause tastes and smells. Special sensory cells then send messages through to your brain to be recognized. Your sense of smell is twenty thousand times stronger than your sense of taste! Often what you think you are tasting you are really just smelling.

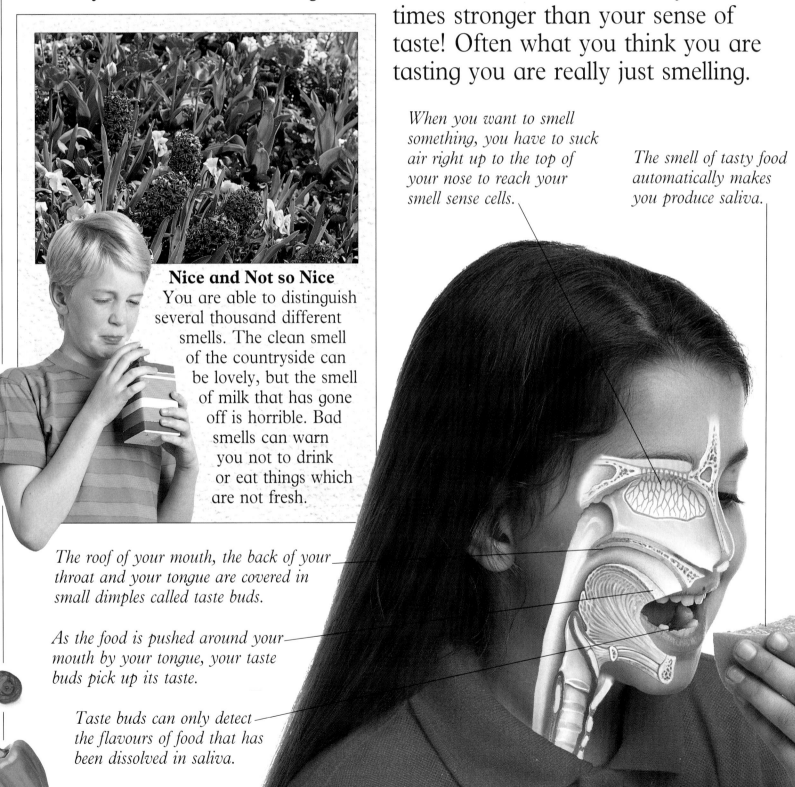

Nice and Not so Nice
You are able to distinguish several thousand different smells. The clean smell of the countryside can be lovely, but the smell of milk that has gone off is horrible. Bad smells can warn you not to drink or eat things which are not fresh.

When you want to smell something, you have to suck air right up to the top of your nose to reach your smell sense cells.

The smell of tasty food automatically makes you produce saliva.

The roof of your mouth, the back of your throat and your tongue are covered in small dimples called taste buds.

As the food is pushed around your mouth by your tongue, your taste buds pick up its taste.

Taste buds can only detect the flavours of food that has been dissolved in saliva.

Trick your Taste Buds

When you eat something, your sense of smell helps you to get the flavour. Block your nose and taste carrot and cucumber. It is hard to tell the difference between them. If you hold a piece of onion under someone's nose and give them mashed apple to eat they think they are eating onion. This is why you cannot taste your food properly when you have a cold.

Coffee grains are bitter

Lemon is sour

Kippers are salty

Honey is sweet

Still Hungry?

The look of food is important as well as its taste and smell – pink sweetcorn still tastes like sweetcorn, but would you want to eat it?

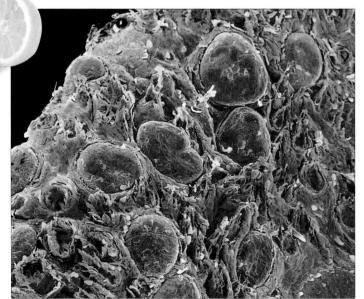

Busy Buds

If you look at a tongue through a strong magnifying glass you can see lots of bumps. Around the base of these bumps there are taste buds. Inside them there are special cells which sense taste.

Tongue Map

There are four sorts of taste buds. Each type is on a different part of your tongue and can detect a different taste. The four tastes are salty, sweet, bitter and sour.

TEETH

You use your teeth to break up food into pieces that are small enough to swallow. Some are shaped for biting and others for chewing. You have two sets of teeth. The first set are called milk teeth and there are 20 of them. At the age of about six, you start to lose your milk teeth. One by one the second set, the 32 adult teeth, grow in their place. Teeth are strong and keep working for many years.

Gappy Grin
Children are left with gaps where their milk teeth have fallen out and they are waiting for their adult teeth to grow.

Cases for Braces
Sometimes teeth grow crookedly or become overcrowded in the mouth. Often this can be put right by wearing teeth braces.

Healthy gums are just as important as healthy teeth – they help to hold your teeth in place.

Still Rooted
This skull shows how teeth are rooted into the two powerful jawbones.

Complete Set
A full set of adult teeth has eight incisors, four canines, eight premolars and twelve molars. Four of the molars are called wisdom teeth.

Jawbone

Incisors   Canine   Premolar   Molars

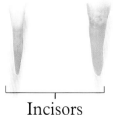

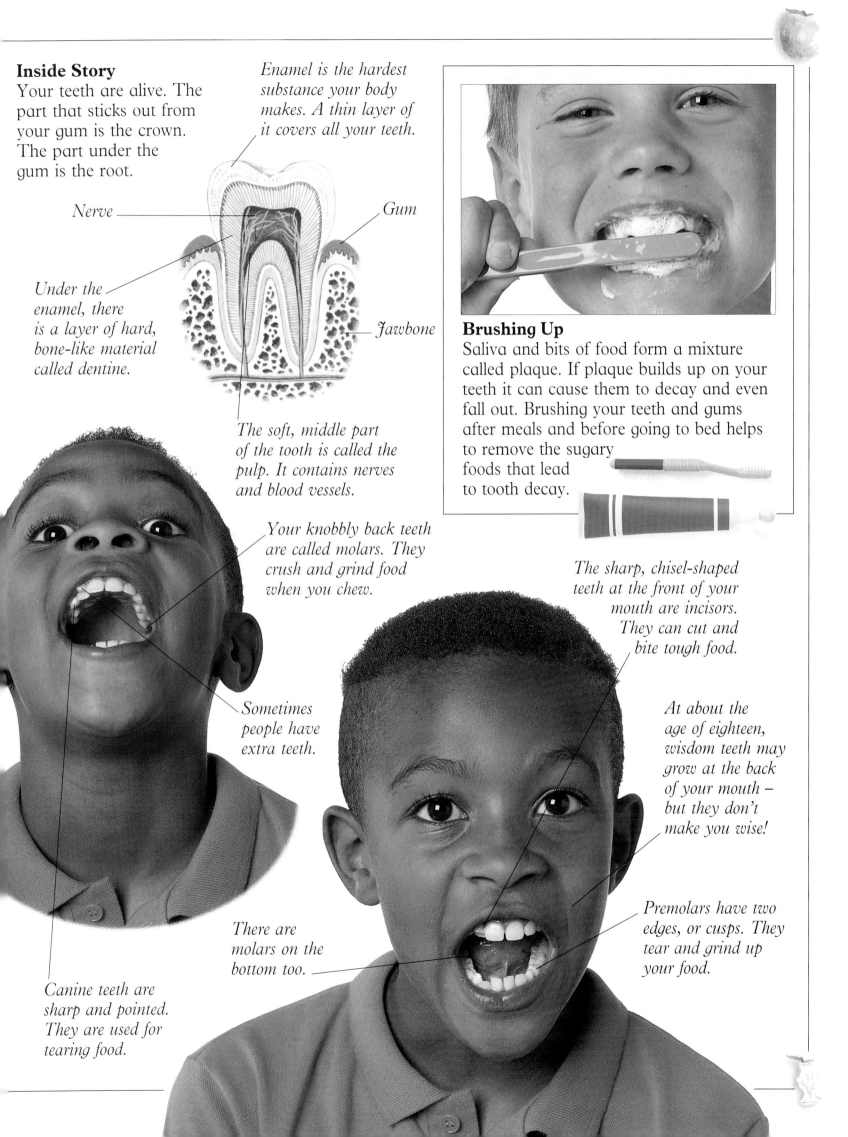

Inside Story
Your teeth are alive. The part that sticks out from your gum is the crown. The part under the gum is the root.

Enamel is the hardest substance your body makes. A thin layer of it covers all your teeth.

Nerve

Gum

Under the enamel, there is a layer of hard, bone-like material called dentine.

Jawbone

The soft, middle part of the tooth is called the pulp. It contains nerves and blood vessels.

Brushing Up
Saliva and bits of food form a mixture called plaque. If plaque builds up on your teeth it can cause them to decay and even fall out. Brushing your teeth and gums after meals and before going to bed helps to remove the sugary foods that lead to tooth decay.

Your knobbly back teeth are called molars. They crush and grind food when you chew.

The sharp, chisel-shaped teeth at the front of your mouth are incisors. They can cut and bite tough food.

Sometimes people have extra teeth.

At about the age of eighteen, wisdom teeth may grow at the back of your mouth – but they don't make you wise!

There are molars on the bottom too.

Premolars have two edges, or cusps. They tear and grind up your food.

Canine teeth are sharp and pointed. They are used for tearing food.

EATING

Food is the fuel that provides energy for your body. The energy is measured in units called kilojoules. Before your body can use the food you eat, it has to be broken down into tiny bits that are small enough to pass into your blood. This digestion takes about 24 hours, as the food flows through a long tube winding all the way from your mouth to your bottom.

Squashed Insides
The small intestine is tightly coiled up inside your tummy.

1 Food starts being digested in your mouth. Your spit, or saliva, has a digestive juice which starts to break down the food.

Your liver is a 'chemical factory'. It also stores vitamins.

Windpipe

2 The food travels down a foodpipe, called the gullet.

3 Your stomach is a thick bag. Food is churned up inside it and mixed with strong stomach juices to make a kind of soup.

4 After leaving your stomach, your food flows down your small intestine. Goodness from the food seeps through the thin walls into your blood.

Large intestine

Small intestine

Fats

Minerals

Vitamins

Proteins

Get into Groups!
Foods can be put into groups. Fats and carbohydrates provide you with energy. Vitamins and minerals keep you healthy. Proteins build cells and so help your body to grow and repair itself.

5 Your large intestine holds the food that your body cannot digest. Later it is passed out of your body through your rectum.

6 Your bladder stores urine. When it fills up you feel the need to go to the toilet to empty it.

A Lump in the Throat

You can swallow even if you are standing on your head! This is because your food does not slide down through you – it is squeezed along by muscles in your digestive tube. This is called peristalsis and it happens all the time, without you having to think about it. The muscles of a snake can squeeze an egg through its body in the same way.

Sleeping uses about 275 kilojoules an hour

Walking uses about 1000 kilojoules an hour

Drawing uses about 350 kilojoules an hour

Netball and other vigorous sports use about 2300 kilojoules an hour

You have two kidneys. Each one is about the size of your clenched fist.

Fuel Burning

If a car travels very fast it uses up more fuel than if it goes slowly. The same is true of your body. When you exercise you use up more kilojoules than when you are asleep.

Narrow tubes, called ureters, take urine from the kidneys to the bladder.

Carbohydrates

Any water your body does not need is turned into urine by your kidneys.

How Long?

If you could stretch your whole digestive system out in a straight line it would be about as long as ten metre rules!

MUSCLES

Try to sit as still as you can. Is anything moving?
Even when you think you are completely still,
many parts of your body are moving.
Your heart is beating and your
intestines and lungs are
working. All these
movements are made by
muscles. You have over 600
muscles spread throughout your
body. Every bend, stretch, twist
and turn you make depends on
them. You use about 200 muscles
each time you take a step, and
many more when you jump.

*Your brain sends
messages to your
muscles and makes
them move.*

*The largest muscle
in your body is the
gluteus maximus
muscle in your
thigh and bottom.*

*If you stand on
tiptoe, you can see
your calf muscles in
the back of your leg.*

Muscle Food
To keep your muscles working
properly you need a diet that
includes protein. Foods which are
full of protein include eggs, cheese
and dried beans.

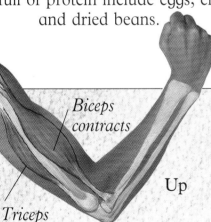

Biceps
contracts

Triceps
relaxes

Up

Biceps
relaxes

Down

Triceps contracts

Arm Bend
Muscles are attached to bones and
make them move. But they can only
pull, they cannot push – which is why
they always work in pairs. In your
arm, the biceps and triceps muscles
work together to move it up and down.
When the biceps pulls, or contracts,
it gets shorter and fatter
and bends the arm.
As the biceps pulls, the
triceps muscle relaxes.

*Before you begin to
make any strenuous
movements you should
always warm up your
muscles by doing gentle
loosening-up and
stretching exercises.*

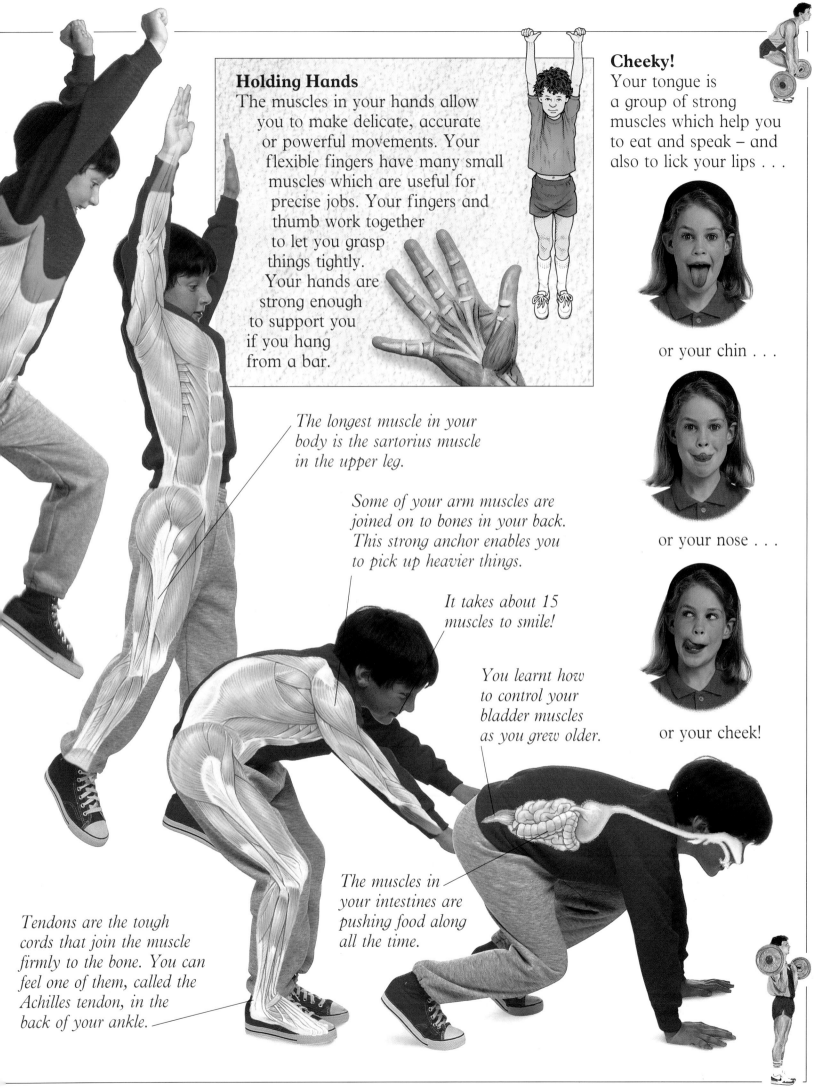

Holding Hands

The muscles in your hands allow you to make delicate, accurate or powerful movements. Your flexible fingers have many small muscles which are useful for precise jobs. Your fingers and thumb work together to let you grasp things tightly. Your hands are strong enough to support you if you hang from a bar.

Cheeky!

Your tongue is a group of strong muscles which help you to eat and speak – and also to lick your lips . . .

or your chin . . .

or your nose . . .

or your cheek!

The longest muscle in your body is the sartorius muscle in the upper leg.

Some of your arm muscles are joined on to bones in your back. This strong anchor enables you to pick up heavier things.

It takes about 15 muscles to smile!

You learnt how to control your bladder muscles as you grew older.

The muscles in your intestines are pushing food along all the time.

Tendons are the tough cords that join the muscle firmly to the bone. You can feel one of them, called the Achilles tendon, in the back of your ankle.

SKELETON

Without a frame to support your body you would collapse, lose your shape and be unable to move. Your body's frame is called a skeleton. It gives your body strength and it protects the soft parts inside. Your skeleton is made up of more than 200 bones. They are light enough to allow you to move about easily and they have joints so that you can bend your body to do many things.

You have twelve pairs of ribs. They are all joined to a row of bones in your back called your spine.

From the side, your spine looks curved, like the letter S. It helps you to stand up straight.

Ulna

Femur

A Tall Order
Your bones keep growing until you are in your early 20's. You cannot change your height – it is decided in your genes and passed on from your parents. But you are about one centimetre shorter in the evening than you are in the morning! This is because the pads of cartilage in your spine get squashed as you walk about all day.

Yes and No Bones
The bones of your spine are called vertebrae. The top two vertebrae, the atlas and axis, fit together to allow your head to nod and to move from side to side.

Atlas

Axis

Your nose is not made of bone but of rubbery material, called cartilage. If you look at a skeleton you will not see a nose bone, only nose holes.

Radius

Fibula

Tibia

Your ankle is a joint. It is made up of bones in the foot and the ends of the leg bones, the tibia and fibula.

Soft Centre

Some animals, like this crab, do not have a skeleton inside them. Instead, they have a hard outer covering, called an exoskeleton.

Inside Information

Your bones are all hidden inside your body. So if doctors want to look at them, they have to take special photographs, called X-rays. The X-ray camera can see straight through your skin and show what the bones look like. On this X-ray of a hand, you can see that one of the bones in the little finger is broken.

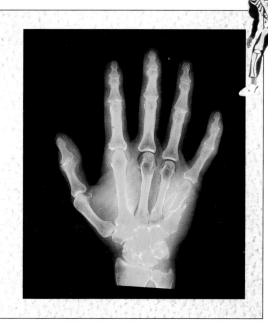

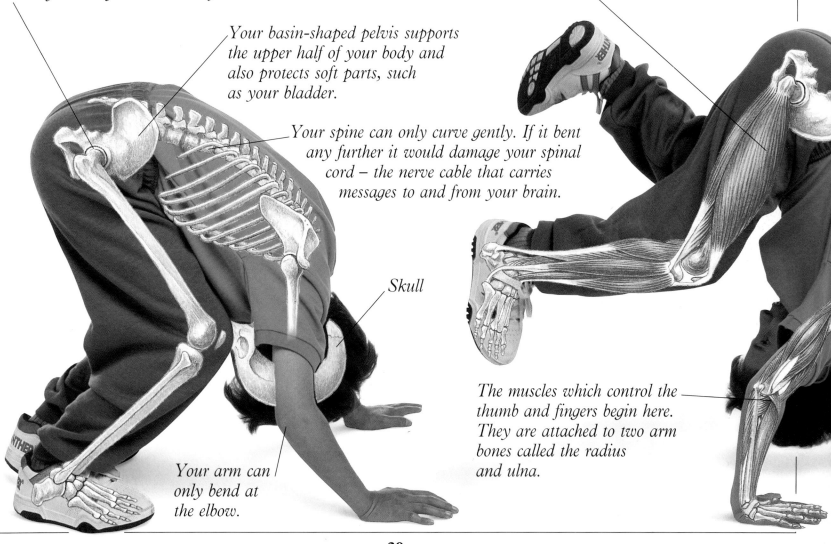

Your hip joint is where the end of the thigh bone, or femur, fits into a socket in your pelvis. This joint helps you to bend your body almost in half.

Bones give muscles a place to hang on to, but without these muscles, the bones would not be able to move. Muscle power is transferred to the bones along strong bands called tendons.

Your basin-shaped pelvis supports the upper half of your body and also protects soft parts, such as your bladder.

Your spine can only curve gently. If it bent any further it would damage your spinal cord – the nerve cable that carries messages to and from your brain.

Skull

Your arm can only bend at the elbow.

The muscles which control the thumb and fingers begin here. They are attached to two arm bones called the radius and ulna.

BONES

Your bones are hard and strong. They are not solid though, so they are not as heavy as you would think. In fact, they only make up 14 per cent of your total body weight – they are lighter than your muscles. Bones are not dead and dry – they are living, and can repair themselves if they break. Your body is made up of lots of bones all working together and linked by joints. If you had no knee joints, you would have to walk with stiff legs.

What's Inside a Bone?

The outer part of all your bones is hard and tough but the inside of many of them is spongy. These lightweight, soft centres are criss-crossed by small struts which make your bones strong, but not too heavy. This idea of strength without weight is copied in buildings such as the Eiffel Tower.

Criss-cross struts

The spongy inner bone looks like a honeycomb.

Blood vessels take oxygen and food to bone cells.

Some bones are filled with jelly-like marrow. Red blood cells are made in the bone marrow.

Your two feet contain one quarter of the bones in your whole body!

Your neck is much shorter than a giraffe's, but it has the same number of vertebrae!

The tiny tail bones at the end of your spine, called the coccyx, protect your spinal cord.

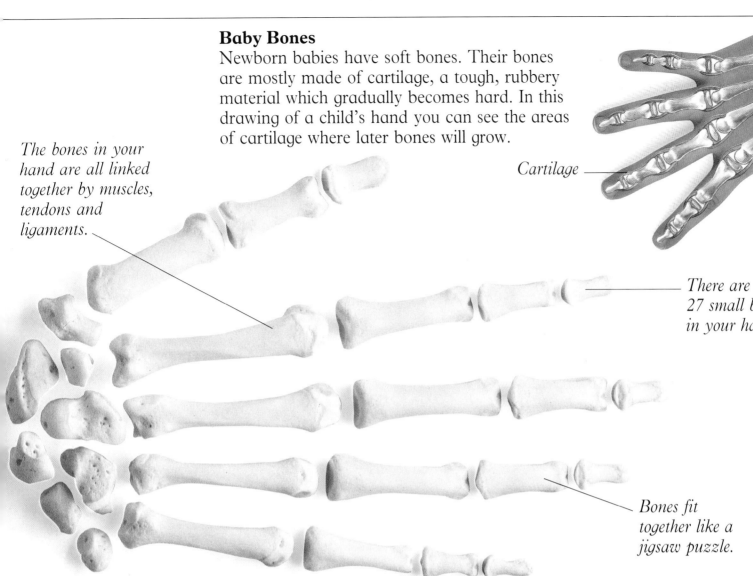

Baby Bones

Newborn babies have soft bones. Their bones are mostly made of cartilage, a tough, rubbery material which gradually becomes hard. In this drawing of a child's hand you can see the areas of cartilage where later bones will grow.

Cartilage

The bones in your hand are all linked together by muscles, tendons and ligaments.

There are 27 small bones in your hand.

Bones fit together like a jigsaw puzzle.

Bone Work

You have three kinds of bone – long bones like those in your legs, short bones such as those in your hand and spine, and flat bones like your shoulder and skull. Bones are linked by different kinds of joints, which allow them to move in different ways.

Your thumb is special. It has a saddle joint in it which allows you to move your thumb in two directions.

You have flat gliding joints in your foot.

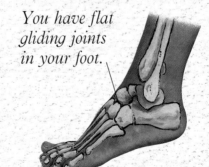

Your kneecap, or patella, protects your knee.

The shoulder has a ball-and-socket joint. The round end of one bone fits into a cup-shaped hole in the other. Your shoulder can move in a complete circle.

Your knee joint, like your elbow, is a hinge joint. The end of one bone fits into a sort of hollow in the other. This kind of joint will only bend in one direction.

ILLNESS AND INJURY

Infections are caused by germs. For much of the time your body is fighting off these harmful germs without you knowing – tears protect your eyes and acids destroy the germs in your stomach. But sometimes your defences are beaten and you fall ill, or you may have an accident and get hurt. Your body then battles to try to make you better.

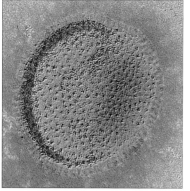

Beware, Bad Germ!
Your body usually resists germs like this flu virus. But if there are lots of them, or if your body is weak, germs get inside your body, multiply and make you ill.

First Aid
Germs can get into your body through a cut. So wounds should be cleaned and covered.

Safety pins for fastening bandages

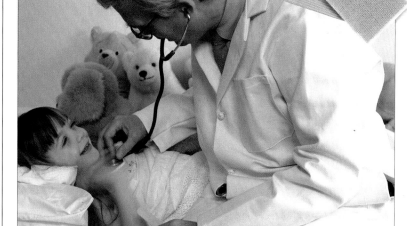

Getting Better
After some infections, such as measles and mumps, your body builds up a resistance, called immunity. You probably will not catch these infections again.

Colds can cause your eyes to water.

Catching a Cold
Minor infections, such as colds, are common. A red, runny nose or a sore, swollen throat are signs that you have caught a cold.

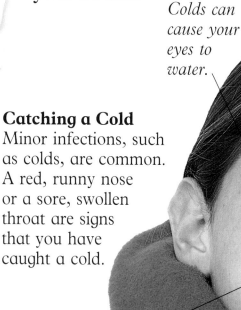

When you have a cold, your nose gets stuffed up with a slimy substance called mucus. This mucus is made from dead white blood cells.

Bandages for covering wounds, and cotton wool for washing or putting on cream

Plaster for covering cuts

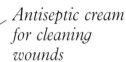

Antiseptic cream for cleaning wounds

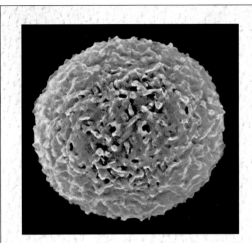

Battling Body

When germs manage to get inside your body, armies of white blood cells rush through your blood to the site of the invasion. Then a fierce battle begins. The white blood cells produce tiny proteins, called antibodies, to help them defeat the germs.

Hold it Right There

If you break a bone it can heal up again because it is alive and can grow new cells to close up the break. Plaster casts keep bones still while they mend.

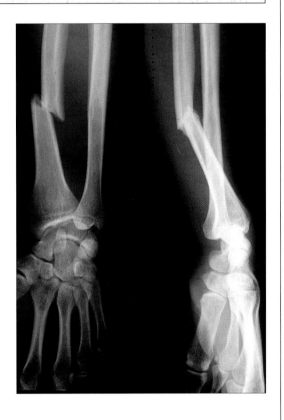

Sick people often get hot, and sweat. The watery sweat dries on your skin and cools you down. You need to drink lots of liquid to replace this lost water.

If you feel tired when you are ill, this is your body telling you that you should rest. You need to save your energy for fighting the germs.

Your body normally has a temperature of about 37 °C. This may rise if you are ill.

Wrapping up warmly may stop your head cold from spreading to your chest and turning into a chesty cough.

Good as New

When you cut yourself your skin and blood seal the hole. Leaks in your skin are repaired quickly so that you do not lose too much blood.

Cells in the blood, called platelets, rush to the wound and stick together to plug the hole.

Strands of a material called fibrin form a 'wall' against germs. This is called a scab.

When the scab drops off, the skin underneath should be almost healed.

WHERE DO I COME FROM?

You began your life as an egg which was only about the size of this full stop.

This tiny fertilized egg grew for about nine months inside your mother before you were born. While a baby is growing, it relies on the mother for everything and although a baby cannot do very much when it is first born, already it is a complete and very special person.

The Beginning

Everyone is made of billions of living units, called cells. A baby starts when an egg cell from a woman and a sperm cell from a man join together to make one new cell. For the egg and sperm to meet, the man and woman must have sexual intercourse. This is sometimes called making love because the man and woman treat each other lovingly. The man's penis gets firm and he puts it into the woman's vagina. He squirts a mixture called semen, which has sperm in it, inside her to join the egg.

Egg tube

Ovary

Egg

Uterus

Vagina

Bladder

Penis

Testes make sperm

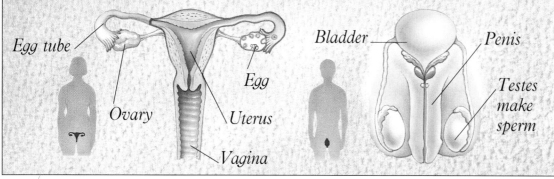

The fertilized egg grows and divides into two.

It divides into four, eight, sixteen, and so on . . .

Sperm are like tiny tadpoles with long tails. They swim to the tube where the egg is waiting. One sperm may then fertilize the egg.

While it is dividing it is travelling to the womb, or uterus.

After about eight weeks the group of cells starts to look more like a baby.

The fingers, toes and face are formed.

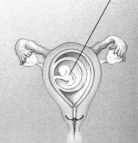

After nine days the egg attaches itself to the wall of the uterus.

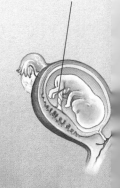

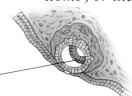

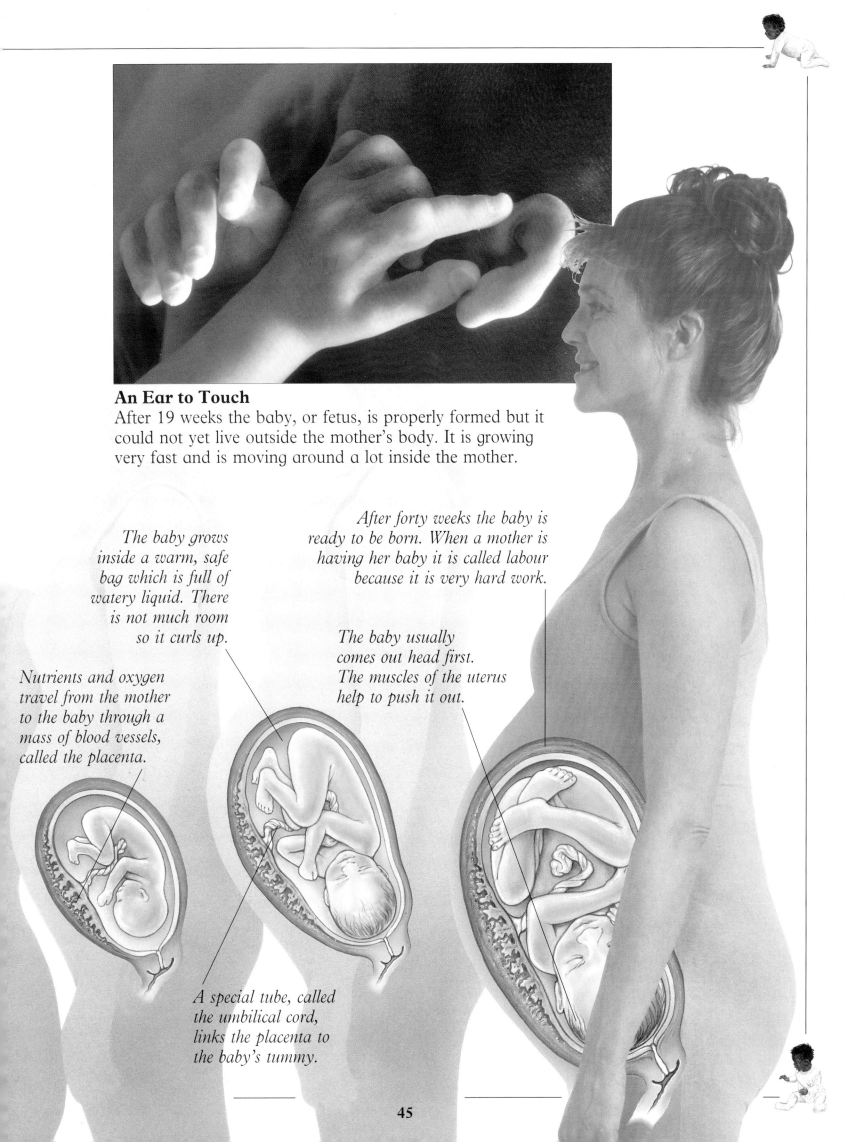

An Ear to Touch

After 19 weeks the baby, or fetus, is properly formed but it could not yet live outside the mother's body. It is growing very fast and is moving around a lot inside the mother.

The baby grows inside a warm, safe bag which is full of watery liquid. There is not much room so it curls up.

After forty weeks the baby is ready to be born. When a mother is having her baby it is called labour because it is very hard work.

Nutrients and oxygen travel from the mother to the baby through a mass of blood vessels, called the placenta.

The baby usually comes out head first. The muscles of the uterus help to push it out.

A special tube, called the umbilical cord, links the placenta to the baby's tummy.

FAMILY LIKENESS

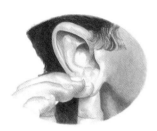

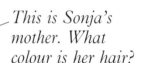

Has anyone ever told you that you look like your parents or grandparents? Because they are older than you, it may be difficult to see the likenesses, but look at photographs of them when they were your age and you may be surprised! You are who you are because of your parents. Some things about you come from your father and some from your mother. This is called heredity. In turn, your parents inherited characteristics from their parents.

Family Ears?

Some features, such as being able to roll your tongue or having attached or unattached earlobes, are passed on in families. Does your family have any of these features?

This photograph of Peter's parents was taken some years ago.

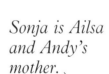

This is Sonja's mother. What colour is her hair?

Sonja writes with her left hand. So does her daughter, Ailsa.

Sonja

Sonja is Ailsa and Andy's mother.

Family Likeness

In this photograph all the people belong to the same family. Can you spot the similarities?

This is a photograph of Peter's grandfather and both of his grandmothers.

Identical twins

Two of a Kind?

There are two types of twins – identical and non-identical. Identical twins grow from one egg. They are always the same sex and look alike. Non-identical twins are from two separate eggs. They are no more alike than brothers and sisters and they may be boys, girls, or one of each.

Non-identical twins

Peter is Ailsa and Andy's father.

A Family Tree

Peter's parents   Sonja's parents

Peter   Sonja

Andy   Ailsa

Pass it On

The instructions for creating a new person are passed in the body cells from parent to child. They are called genes. Half come from the father and half from the mother. You can find out where your genes have come from by drawing a family tree.

Peter

Look at the shape of Ailsa's face and at her nose and her eyes. Does she look like her mother or her father?

Ailsa

Do you think the colour of Andy's hair came from his mother, his father, or perhaps his grandmother?

Is Andy like his mother or his father? Look at his smile.

Andy

GLOSSARY

Artery A blood vessel that carries blood away from your heart to the rest of your body.

Bacteria Microscopic one-cell creatures found all around us. Some are helpful to us; others cause diseases.

Binocular vision Two eyes working together to allow you to judge distance.

Blood vessel A tube that carries blood through your body.

Braille A special alphabet, made up of patterns of raised dots, which allows blind people to read.

Carbohydrates Foods that give us energy.

Carbon dioxide A gas that is produced as a waste product by your body and exhaled via your lungs.

Cartilage The rubbery, slippery material that lines your joints. It stops friction and cushions your bones.

Cell The smallest living unit of your body.

Decibel A unit for measuring noise levels.

Diaphragm The strong, flat muscle which you use when you breathe. It lies just below your lungs.

Digestion The way foods are broken down into tiny pieces to be used as fuel and to build new cells.

Epiglottis A trap door which stops food going into your breathing tubes when you swallow.

Fats Important types of food found in some plants and all animals. When eaten, they give us energy. But eating too much fat is bad for your health.

Genes They carry the instructions that pass on family likeness from both parents to the baby.

Germs Tiny living things that can get into your body and cause illness. Germs include bacteria and viruses. Not all germs are harmful.

Infection A type of illness, such as measles or mumps, which can be caught from other people.

Keratin The tough substance that is found in your hair and nails.

Kilojoules Units used to measure the amount of energy in each kind of food.

Larynx Also called the voice box. It is about half way down your neck and has your vocal cords in it.

Ligaments Tough, ropy bands that hold your bones together at your joints.

Nerves Threads of cells, which carry messages between your brain and the rest of your body.

Nutrients Basic substances found in food. Your body uses them for fuel, growth and repair.

Proteins Substances found in your food. They help to form cells and so build and repair your body.

Pulse The throbbing of your arteries caused by the beating of your heart. Your pulse can be felt most easily on the edge of your wrist.

Reflex A movement that happens without thought, such as instantly dropping something that is hot.

Saliva A liquid made in your throat that helps to break down food. It also enables you to taste your food.

Signing A way of talking by moving your hands. It is used by deaf people.

Tendons Strong bands that connect muscles to bones.

Trachea A tube which leads from the larynx to the bronchial tubes in the chest. It is also called the windpipe.

Urine Waste water and other chemicals that pass out of your body.

Vaccination The swallowing, or injection, of a substance that will provide your body with immunity against disease.

Vein A blood vessel that carries blood to your heart.

Vertebrae Bones that link together to form your spine.

Vitamins and Minerals Groups of substances found in food. You need them to keep you healthy.

Vocal cords Two ligaments which stretch across your larynx. They vibrate as air passes over them and this allows you to speak.

X-rays Invisible rays that pass through objects. X-ray photographs show the inside of your body.

Acknowledgments

Photography: Steve Gorton, Tim Ridley and Andy Crawford.

Illustrations: Norman Barber, Joanna Cameron, Tony Graham, Kaye Hodges, Norman Lacey, Janos Marffy, Annabel Milne and Sean Milne.

Thanks to: Truly Scrumptious Child Model Agency and Scallywags.

t – **top**   l – **left**   r – **right**

INDEX